# Silent Swoop

## An Owl, an Egg, and a Warm Shirt Pocket

By Michelle Houts    Illustrated by Deb Hoeffner

Dawn Publications

*To Flannery, for the story, and to Cis, for the facts, with gratitude. ⇀ MH*

*I dedicate this book to all creatures great and small and to those who treasure their specialness. ⇀ DH*

## Acknowledgments

I'm grateful to the current and former staff of the World Bird Sanctuary for their assistance in uncovering Coal's story. Special thanks to Brian Crawford for sharing his father's journey and to Thomas Rollins for the photographs. — Michelle Houts

### Library of Congress Cataloging-in-Publication Data

Names: Houts, Michelle, author. | Hoeffner, Deb, illustrator.
Title: Silent swoop : an owl, an egg, and a warm shirt pocket / by Michelle
  Houts ; illustrated by Deb Hoeffner.
Description: First edition. | Nevada City, CA : Dawn Publications, [2019] |
  Audience: Ages 4-9. | Audience: K to grade 3.
Identifiers: LCCN 2018046403| ISBN 9781584696469 (hardcover) | ISBN
  9781584696476 (pbk.)
Subjects: LCSH: Crawford, Walter, 1945-2015--Juvenile literature. | Great
  horned owl--Juvenile literature. | Human-animal relationships--Juvenile
  literature. | Wildlife rescue--Juvenile literature. | Wildlife
  conservation--Juvenile literature.
Classification: LCC QL696.S83 H68 2019 | DDC 598.9/7--dc23 LC record
available at https://lccn.loc.gov/2018046403

Book design and computer production by
Patty Arnold, *Menagerie Design and Publishing*
Cover font: Beau Rivage
Interior font: Windsor
Illustrations: watercolor and pastels
Manufactured by Regent Publishing Services, Hong Kong
Printed July, 2019, in ShenZhen, Guangdong, China
10 9 8 7 6 5 4 3 2 1
First Edition

## Dawn Publications

12402 Bitney Springs Road
Nevada City, CA 95959
800-545-7475
www.dawnpub.com

In the dark of night, no one saw the Great Horned Owl glide over the coal yard. Not a soul was around as powerful, silent wings propelled her over sleepy machines and shadowy mounds of coal.

Nobody noticed when she landed under a conveyor belt and settled into the dust.

When the morning
sun pushed the darkness
aside, she was long gone.
What she left behind would
cause quite a stir in the coal
yard that day.

Workers crouched low to get a closer
look. The foreman scratched his
head. There was work to be
done. But if the conveyor
belt moved, the eggs would
be crushed.

The workers called Walter. He knew a lot about birds.
He knew a lot about eggs, too. But even Walter was puzzled
when he peered beneath the conveyor belt. What could he
do? He couldn't leave the eggs in harm's way.

So Walter placed the dusty eggs carefully in his shirt
pocket and went back to work —

back to his bird sanctuary.

Out of the shirt pocket and into an incubator
went the two eggs. Would they hatch?
Walter wasn't very hopeful.

Day after day,
Walter watched.
He wondered.
He waited.

One day, one of the eggs began to tremble.
With a whole lot of pushing and straining, stretching and crackling, the egg opened and a fuzzy white owlet peered out. Walter was delighted. "Hello, Coal," he said.

Coal looked at Walter with big, round eyes. Then, Walter and Coal waited together. They watched. But the second egg didn't hatch. There would be no brother or sister for little Coal.

Walter sighed. "And that's the way it goes, sometimes."

Little Coal grew. Coal was relaxed and calm with his caregivers. They made sure he knew he was an owl, not a human. He learned to eat like a Great Horned Owl. He found his voice and began to hoot like a Great Horned Owl.

Hoo-h'HOO-hoo-hoo!

Coal hooted at his own reflection. And he always hooted at Walter.

Hoo-h'HOO-hoo-hoo!

As Coal grew, his white fuzz was replaced with long gray-brown feathers. His tufts stood tall and his beak grew curved and black.

Because he was so calm, Walter and his crew wondered: Could Coal be the perfect bird to help others learn about Great Horned Owls? Maybe. But first he had a lot to learn.

The world was full of noisy children,
and balloons,
   and strollers.

Coal went everywhere with his trainers
so that he could get used to people.
He even went home with them on
the weekends. His trainers always
made sure he felt safe.

And Coal did feel safe—except when he saw an opossum, a snake, or a dog.

When that happened, Coal's tufts would stand straight in the air, and he'd stay very still.

Coal was fond of most people, but he especially loved Walter. Whenever Walter appeared, Coal puffed out his beard and stretched out his tail and called out loudly.

Coal loved Walter so much, he'd offer him the mouse right from his mouth.

When Coal and his trainers traveled to zoos, he would sit quietly on a trainer's glove.

He went to schools, where he was the star of the show, blinking and watching the children.

He visited nursing homes, where he sat with the residents in peaceful silence.

One night, while Coal was safe and comfortable at the sanctuary, something was happening back at the coal yard. In the dark of night, no one saw the Great Horned Owl glide over the coal yard. Not a soul was around as powerful, silent wings propelled her over sleepy machines and shadowy mounds of coal.

Nobody noticed when she landed under a conveyor belt
and settled into the dust.

When the phone rang, Walter couldn't believe his ears.

There was another egg beneath the conveyor belt at the power plant.

Once again, Walter waited. Would the egg hatch?
This time Walter was a little more hopeful.
He watched.
He wondered.
He waited.

And then one day a fuzzy white owlet named Junior greeted the world with big eyes. Coal had a brother after all!

Walter smiled. "And, that's the way it goes, sometimes."

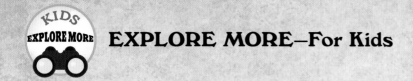

# Great Horned Owl

## What's in a Name?

Those aren't horns on top of its head. And they're not ears, either. They're tufts of feathers.

## Night Vision

Big eyes help an owl see at night. But its eyes don't move like ours do. An owl must turn its head to see in different directions. Great Horned Owls can turn their heads almost completely around (about 270 degrees).

## Silent Swoop

Great Horned Owls are almost silent when they fly. Their broad wings allow them to glide without flapping. When they do flap, the noise is muffled by special feathers on their wings.

## Grasp and Grip

An owl's sharp claws are called *talons*. A Great Horned Owl uses its strong talons to strike, grasp, and carry prey.

## Bird of Prey

A Great Horned Owl is one of the most common owls in North America. It's also one of the largest owls. It's called a *bird of prey* because it hunts animals for its food. Its favorite meals include mice, rabbits, small mammals, and birds. It even eats skunks!

Although opossums and snakes frightened Coal, they are natural prey for a wild Great Horned Owl.

## Listen Up

A Great Horned Owl can hear a mouse moving in the weeds at a distance of 75 feet (23 meters)—in the dark! Its ears are openings hidden under the dark feathers on either side of its face.

# The Man Who Saved Coal

Coal's story had a happy ending because of Walter Crawford. Walter wanted to take care of sick and injured birds, especially birds of prey. He started caring for a few birds in his basement. His project grew to become the World Bird Sanctuary. During his lifetime, Walter helped thousands of birds and won many awards for his work.

**Walter Crawford**

**Coal**

The sanctuary takes care of birds and also teaches people about them. Coal and Junior became education birds. They helped many children and adults understand and appreciate Great Horned Owls.

*Photos by Thomas Rollins Photography*

## Nests and Eggs

Great Horned Owls typically nest in trees. Instead of building their own nest, they use an old nest made by other birds, often a hawk's. Sometimes they use tree hollows, cliff ledges, deserted buildings, or human-made platforms. Sometimes they will nest on the ground.

A female usually lays one egg at a time, a few days apart, so Coal's mother must have visited the coal yard at least twice before Coal's egg was found. Coal's egg was laid over thirty years ago. Junior's egg came either one or two years later. Because the eggs were found in the same nesting spot, they probably had the same mother.

*Actual Size*

# Writing Coal's Story

I first heard about Coal from my daughter's college roommate, who had been an intern at the World Bird Sanctuary. Coal's story was unique in so many ways, but most especially because he was rescued as an egg! After many emails and phone calls I found someone who was able to share more about Coal. But she was busy, and I was too, so I put Coal's story on hold. Still, I couldn't help but think of Coal often.

Then, I took a master class with renowned authors Jane Yolen and Heidi Stemple. At the end of the class Jane asked the question: "What's the story you wanted to tell but didn't?" Immediately, I knew it was Coal's story! I talked to my contact at the sanctuary and learned that Coal had passed away earlier that same week—at just about the same time Jane was nudging me to tell his tale. I knew I needed to finish what I'd started. I needed to tell the world about Walter and Coal.

# Finding the Facts

Coal's story has been told and retold over the years with many different twists and turns. Record-keeping more than thirty years ago was done by hand, and sometimes scribbled notes were misplaced or never filed. The year and the exact location of the power plant were not recorded, but everyone agrees that Coal's egg arrived at the World Bird Sanctuary in St. Louis, Missouri, in Walter Crawford's shirt pocket.

The facts of Coal's story told here come from the first-hand accounts of his caregivers, but some anecdotal information was added; for example, we don't know exactly what Walter said when Coal and Junior were born. Learn more facts about Walter and the World Bird Sanctuary at www.worldbirdsanctuary.org.

# Literacy Connection: Read Aloud Tips

1. Read the title and look at the cover illustration. Identify the names of the author and illustrator. Ask *What do you think the story is about?*

2. Read the story all the way through, pausing to explain unfamiliar words if necessary. You may need to pause after the first page to explain that power plants make electricity from coal. The coal moves from a coal yard along a conveyor belt into the plant.

3. When finished, ask *Was your prediction correct? What was the book about?*

4. Explain that the story is true. Coal and Junior were real birds. Walter was a real person who rescued them. Read or paraphrase "Writing Coal's Story" and "Finding the Facts."

5. Discuss the differences between fiction and nonfiction. This story has some of both. Then read aloud the nonfiction information and look at the photos on the "Explore More for Kids" pages.

6. Read the story again. Note that when one of the eggs doesn't hatch at the beginning of the story, Walter says, "And that's the way it goes sometimes." He says the same thing at the end of the story. Discuss what he means each time he says it. (Sometimes wildlife rescues are successful and sometimes they're not. In nature, some eggs hatch and some eggs don't.) Discuss how the same words can evoke different feelings depending on the context of the story.

7. Follow-up by creating a KWL Chart about owls and doing the suggested STEM activities.